NEVER A DULL MOMENT

∽ ⌇ ∾

STUFF MY KID SAID & DID

PETER PAUPER PRESS, INC.
RYE BROOK, NEW YORK

PETER PAUPER PRESS
Fine Books and Gifts Since 1928

Our Company

In 1928, at the age of twenty-two, Peter Beilenson began printing books on a small press in the basement of his parents' home in Larchmont, New York. Peter—and later, his wife, Edna—sought to create fine books that sold at "prices even a pauper could afford."

Today, still family owned and operated, Peter Pauper Press continues to honor our founders' legacy—and our customers' expectations—of beauty, quality, and value.

Designed by Heather Zschock
Copyright © 2018
Peter Pauper Press, Inc.
3 International Drive
Rye Brook, NY 10573 USA
All rights reserved
ISBN 978-1-4413-2801-4
Printed in China
14 13 12 11 10 9

Visit us at www.peterpauper.com

LIFE WITH KIDS...

This **keepsake journal** is for those almost-too-brilliant moments: the parts of your kids' lives you want to capture and remember forever (or help them remember when they're older) in the midst of your busy life. Use the prompts on each page to write down who said or did what—and when and where. Reach for this book whenever your kids discover something new about the world, when they do something hilarious, or when they say something incredible and profound. Your family motto may be "never a dull moment," and this journal will help capture for posterity all the moments that shine.

KID: AGE:

PLACE:

WHAT THEY SAID OR DID:

DATE:

KID: AGE:

PLACE:

WHAT THEY SAID OR DID:

DATE:

KID: AGE:

PLACE:

WHAT THEY SAID OR DID:

DATE:

KID: AGE:

PLACE:

WHAT THEY SAID OR DID:

DATE:

KID: AGE:

PLACE:

WHAT THEY SAID OR DID:

DATE:

KID: AGE:

PLACE:

WHAT THEY SAID OR DID:

DATE:

KID: AGE:

PLACE:

WHAT THEY SAID OR DID:

DATE:

KID: _____ AGE: _____

PLACE: _____

WHAT THEY SAID OR DID: _____

_____

_____

_____

DATE: _____

KID: _____ AGE: _____

PLACE: _____

WHAT THEY SAID OR DID: _____

_____

_____

_____

DATE: _____

KID: AGE:

PLACE:

WHAT THEY SAID OR DID:

DATE:

KID: .... AGE: ....

PLACE: ....

WHAT THEY SAID OR DID: ....

....

....

....

....

....

....

....

....

....

DATE:

KID: AGE:

PLACE:

WHAT THEY SAID OR DID:

DATE:

KID: AGE:

PLACE:

WHAT THEY SAID OR DID:

DATE:

KID: .... AGE: ....

PLACE: ....

WHAT THEY SAID OR DID:

....

....

....

....

....

....

KID: .... AGE: ....

PLACE: ....

WHAT THEY SAID OR DID: ....

....

....

....

....

....

....

....

KID: AGE:

PLACE:

WHAT THEY SAID OR DID:

DATE:

KID: AGE:

PLACE:

WHAT THEY SAID OR DID:

DATE:

KID: AGE:

PLACE:

WHAT THEY SAID OR DID:

DATE:

KID: AGE:

PLACE:

WHAT THEY SAID OR DID:

DATE:

KID: AGE:

PLACE:

WHAT THEY SAID OR DID:

DATE:

KID: AGE:

PLACE:

WHAT THEY SAID OR DID:

DATE:

KID: AGE:

PLACE:

WHAT THEY SAID OR DID:

DATE:

KID: AGE:

PLACE:

WHAT THEY SAID OR DID:

DATE:

KID: AGE:

PLACE:

WHAT THEY SAID OR DID:

DATE:

KID: AGE:

PLACE:

WHAT THEY SAID OR DID:

DATE:

KID: _____ AGE: _____

PLACE: _____

WHAT THEY SAID OR DID: _____

_____

_____

_____

_____

_____

_____

_____

_____

_____

DATE: _____

KID: AGE:

PLACE:

WHAT THEY SAID OR DID:

DATE:

KID: .... AGE: ....

PLACE: ....

WHAT THEY SAID OR DID: ....

....

....

....

DATE: ....

KID: .... AGE: ....

PLACE: ....

WHAT THEY SAID OR DID: ....

....

....

....

DATE: ....

KID: AGE:

PLACE:

WHAT THEY SAID OR DID:

DATE:

KID: .... AGE: ....

PLACE: ....

WHAT THEY SAID OR DID:
....

....

....

....

....

....

....

....

....

....

DATE: ....

KID: AGE:

PLACE:

WHAT THEY SAID OR DID:

DATE:

KID: AGE:

PLACE:

WHAT THEY SAID OR DID:

DATE:

KID: AGE:

PLACE:

WHAT THEY SAID OR DID:

KID: AGE:

PLACE:

WHAT THEY SAID OR DID:

KID: AGE:

PLACE:

WHAT THEY SAID OR DID:

DATE:

KID: AGE:

PLACE:

WHAT THEY SAID OR DID:

DATE:

KID: AGE:

PLACE:

WHAT THEY SAID OR DID:

DATE:

KID: .... AGE: ....

PLACE: ....

WHAT THEY SAID OR DID: ....

....

....

....

....

....

....

....

....

....

DATE: ....

KID: AGE:

PLACE:

WHAT THEY SAID OR DID:

DATE:

KID: AGE:

PLACE:

WHAT THEY SAID OR DID:

DATE:

KID: AGE:

PLACE:

WHAT THEY SAID OR DID:

DATE:

KID: AGE:

PLACE:

WHAT THEY SAID OR DID:

DATE:

KID: AGE:

PLACE:

WHAT THEY SAID OR DID:

DATE:

KID: AGE:

PLACE:

WHAT THEY SAID OR DID:

DATE:

KID: AGE:

PLACE:

WHAT THEY SAID OR DID:

DATE:

KID: .... AGE: ....

PLACE: ....

WHAT THEY SAID OR DID: ....

....

....

....

....

....

....

DATE: ....

KID: _____ AGE: _____

PLACE: _____

WHAT THEY SAID OR DID: _____

_____

_____

_____

DATE: _____

KID: _____ AGE: _____

PLACE: _____

WHAT THEY SAID OR DID: _____

_____

_____

_____

DATE: _____

KID: AGE:

PLACE:

WHAT THEY SAID OR DID:

DATE:

KID: _____ AGE: _____

PLACE: _____

WHAT THEY SAID OR DID: _____

_____

_____

_____

_____

_____

_____

_____

_____

_____

DATE: _____

KID: AGE:

PLACE:

WHAT THEY SAID OR DID:

DATE:

KID: AGE:

PLACE:

WHAT THEY SAID OR DID:

DATE:

KID: AGE:

PLACE:

WHAT THEY SAID OR DID:

DATE:

KID: _____ AGE: _____

PLACE: _____

WHAT THEY SAID OR DID: _____

_____

_____

_____

_____

_____

_____

_____

_____

_____

_____

DATE: _____

KID: AGE:

PLACE:

WHAT THEY SAID OR DID:

DATE:

KID: _____ AGE: _____

PLACE: _____

WHAT THEY SAID OR DID: _____

_____

_____

_____

_____

_____

_____

DATE: _____

KID: **AGE:**

PLACE:

WHAT THEY SAID OR DID:

DATE:

KID: **AGE:**

PLACE:

WHAT THEY SAID OR DID:

DATE:

KID: AGE:

PLACE:

WHAT THEY SAID OR DID:

DATE:

KID: AGE:

PLACE:

WHAT THEY SAID OR DID:

DATE:

KID: .... AGE: ....

PLACE: ....

WHAT THEY SAID OR DID: ....

....

....

....

....

....

....

....

....

....

....

DATE: ....

KID: .... AGE: ....

PLACE: ....

WHAT THEY SAID OR DID: ....

....

....

....

....

....

....

DATE: ....

KID: .... AGE: ....

PLACE: ....

WHAT THEY SAID OR DID: ....
....
....
....
....

DATE: ....

KID: .... AGE: ....

PLACE: ....

WHAT THEY SAID OR DID: ....
....
....
....
....

DATE: ....

KID: AGE:

PLACE:

WHAT THEY SAID OR DID:

DATE:

KID: AGE:

PLACE:

WHAT THEY SAID OR DID:

DATE:

KID: .... AGE: ....

PLACE: ....

WHAT THEY SAID OR DID: ....

....

....

....

....

....

....

....

....

....

....

....

DATE: ....

KID: .... AGE: ....

PLACE: ....

WHAT THEY SAID OR DID:
....

....

....

....

....

....

....

....

....

....

DATE: ....

KID: _____ AGE: _____

PLACE: _____

WHAT THEY SAID OR DID:

_____

_____

_____

_____

_____

KID: _____ AGE: _____

PLACE: _____

WHAT THEY SAID OR DID:

_____

_____

_____

_____

_____

_____

_____

KID: AGE:

PLACE:

WHAT THEY SAID OR DID:

DATE:

KID: AGE:

PLACE:

WHAT THEY SAID OR DID:

DATE:

KID: AGE:

PLACE:

WHAT THEY SAID OR DID:

DATE:

KID: .... AGE: ....

PLACE: ....

WHAT THEY SAID OR DID: ....

....

....

....

....

....

....

....

....

....

DATE: ....

KID: AGE:

PLACE:

WHAT THEY SAID OR DID:

DATE:

KID: AGE:

PLACE:

WHAT THEY SAID OR DID:

DATE:

KID: AGE:

PLACE:

WHAT THEY SAID OR DID:

DATE:

KID: AGE:

PLACE:

WHAT THEY SAID OR DID:

DATE:

KID: AGE:

PLACE:

WHAT THEY SAID OR DID:

DATE:

KID: AGE:

PLACE:

WHAT THEY SAID OR DID:

DATE:

KID: .... AGE: ....

PLACE: ....

WHAT THEY SAID OR DID: ....

....

....

....

....

....

....

....

....

....

DATE:

KID: AGE:

PLACE:

WHAT THEY SAID OR DID:

DATE:

KID: AGE:

PLACE:

WHAT THEY SAID OR DID:

DATE:

KID: AGE:

PLACE:

WHAT THEY SAID OR DID:

DATE:

KID: AGE:

PLACE:

WHAT THEY SAID OR DID:

DATE:

KID: _____   AGE: _____

PLACE: _____

WHAT THEY SAID OR DID: _____

_____

_____

_____

_____

_____

_____

_____

_____

_____

_____

DATE: _____

KID: AGE:

PLACE:

WHAT THEY SAID OR DID:

DATE:

KID: AGE:

PLACE:

WHAT THEY SAID OR DID:

DATE:

KID: _____ AGE: _____

PLACE: _____

WHAT THEY SAID OR DID:

KID: _____ AGE: _____

PLACE: _____

WHAT THEY SAID OR DID:

_____

_____

_____

_____

_____

_____

KID: .... AGE: ....

PLACE: ....

WHAT THEY SAID OR DID: ....

....

....

....

DATE: ....

KID: .... AGE: ....

PLACE: ....

WHAT THEY SAID OR DID: ....

....

....

....

DATE: ....

KID: .... AGE: ....

PLACE: ....

WHAT THEY SAID OR DID: ....

....

....

....

....

....

....

....

....

....

DATE: ....

KID: .... AGE: ....

PLACE: ....

WHAT THEY SAID OR DID: ....

....

....

....

....

....

....

....

....

....

DATE: ....

KID: AGE:

PLACE:

WHAT THEY SAID OR DID:

DATE:

KID: .... AGE: ....

PLACE: ....

WHAT THEY SAID OR DID:
....
....
....
....
....
....

DATE: ....

KID: AGE:

PLACE:

WHAT THEY SAID OR DID:

DATE:

KID: AGE:

PLACE:

WHAT THEY SAID OR DID:

DATE:

KID: AGE:

PLACE:

WHAT THEY SAID OR DID:

DATE:

KID: AGE:

PLACE:

WHAT THEY SAID OR DID:

DATE:

KID: AGE:

PLACE:

WHAT THEY SAID OR DID:

DATE:

KID: AGE:

PLACE:

WHAT THEY SAID OR DID:

DATE:

KID: AGE:

PLACE:

WHAT THEY SAID OR DID:

DATE:

KID: AGE:

PLACE:

WHAT THEY SAID OR DID:

DATE:

KID: .... AGE: ....

PLACE: ....

WHAT THEY SAID OR DID: ....

....

....

....

....

....

....

....

....

....

....

DATE:

KID: AGE:

PLACE:

WHAT THEY SAID OR DID:

DATE:

KID: AGE:

PLACE:

WHAT THEY SAID OR DID:

DATE:

KID: .... AGE: ....

PLACE: ....

WHAT THEY SAID OR DID: ....

....

....

....

....

....

....

....

....

....

....

DATE: ....

KID: AGE:

PLACE:

WHAT THEY SAID OR DID:

KID: AGE:

PLACE:

WHAT THEY SAID OR DID:

KID: AGE:

PLACE:

WHAT THEY SAID OR DID:

DATE:

KID: AGE:

PLACE:

WHAT THEY SAID OR DID:

DATE:

KID: AGE:

PLACE:

WHAT THEY SAID OR DID:

DATE:

KID: AGE:

PLACE:

WHAT THEY SAID OR DID:

DATE:

KID: AGE:

PLACE:

WHAT THEY SAID OR DID:

DATE:

KID: _____ AGE: _____

PLACE: _____

WHAT THEY SAID OR DID: _____

_____

_____

_____

_____

_____

DATE: _____

KID: AGE:

PLACE:

WHAT THEY SAID OR DID:

DATE:

KID: AGE:

PLACE:

WHAT THEY SAID OR DID:

DATE:

KID: AGE:

PLACE:

WHAT THEY SAID OR DID:

DATE:

KID: AGE:

PLACE:

WHAT THEY SAID OR DID:

DATE:

KID: AGE:

PLACE:

WHAT THEY SAID OR DID:

DATE:

KID: _____ AGE: _____

PLACE: _____

WHAT THEY SAID OR DID: _____

....

....

....

....

....

....

DATE: _____

KID: AGE:

PLACE:

WHAT THEY SAID OR DID:

DATE:

KID: AGE:

PLACE:

WHAT THEY SAID OR DID:

DATE:

KID: .... AGE: ....

PLACE: ....

WHAT THEY SAID OR DID: ....

....

....

....

....

....

....

....

....

....

DATE: ....

KID: .... AGE: ....

PLACE: ....

WHAT THEY SAID OR DID: ....

....

....

....

....

....

....

....

....

DATE: ....

KID: AGE:

PLACE:

WHAT THEY SAID OR DID:

DATE:

KID: .... AGE: ....

PLACE: ....

WHAT THEY SAID OR DID: ....

....

....

....

....

....

....

....

....

....

DATE: ....

KID: AGE:

PLACE:

WHAT THEY SAID OR DID:

KID: AGE:

PLACE:

WHAT THEY SAID OR DID:

KID: AGE:

PLACE:

WHAT THEY SAID OR DID:

DATE:

KID: AGE:

PLACE:

WHAT THEY SAID OR DID:

DATE:

KID: AGE:

PLACE:

WHAT THEY SAID OR DID:

DATE:

KID: .... AGE: ....

PLACE: ....

WHAT THEY SAID OR DID:
....

....

....

....

....

....

....

....

....

....

DATE: ....

KID: AGE:

PLACE:

WHAT THEY SAID OR DID:

DATE:

KID: AGE:

PLACE:

WHAT THEY SAID OR DID:

DATE:

KID: AGE:

PLACE:

WHAT THEY SAID OR DID:

DATE:

KID: AGE:

PLACE:

WHAT THEY SAID OR DID:

DATE:

KID: AGE:

PLACE:

WHAT THEY SAID OR DID:

DATE:

KID: AGE:

PLACE:

WHAT THEY SAID OR DID:

DATE:

KID: AGE:

PLACE:

WHAT THEY SAID OR DID:

DATE:

KID: _____ AGE: _____

PLACE: _____

WHAT THEY SAID OR DID: _____

....

....

....

....

....

....

....

DATE: _____

KID: AGE:

PLACE:

WHAT THEY SAID OR DID:

DATE:

KID: AGE:

PLACE:

WHAT THEY SAID OR DID:

DATE:

KID: .... AGE: ....

PLACE: ....

WHAT THEY SAID OR DID: ....

....

....

....

....

....

....

....

....

....

....

DATE: ....

KID: AGE:

PLACE:

WHAT THEY SAID OR DID:

DATE:

KID: AGE:

PLACE:

WHAT THEY SAID OR DID:

DATE:

KID: _____ AGE: _____

PLACE: _____

WHAT THEY SAID OR DID: _____

_____

_____

_____

_____

_____

_____

_____

_____

_____

DATE: _____

KID: _____ AGE: _____

PLACE: _____

WHAT THEY SAID OR DID:

_____

_____

_____

_____

_____

_____

DATE:

KID: AGE:

PLACE:

WHAT THEY SAID OR DID:

KID: _____ AGE: _____

PLACE: _____

WHAT THEY SAID OR DID: _____

_____

_____

_____

DATE: _____

KID: _____ AGE: _____

PLACE: _____

WHAT THEY SAID OR DID: _____

_____

_____

_____

DATE: _____

KID: .... AGE: ....

PLACE: ....

WHAT THEY SAID OR DID: ....

....

....

....

....

....

....

....

....

....

....

DATE: ....

KID: .... AGE: ....

PLACE: ....

WHAT THEY SAID OR DID: ....

....

....

....

....

....

....

....

....

....

DATE: ....

KID: _____ AGE: _____

PLACE: _____

WHAT THEY SAID OR DID: _____

_____

_____

_____

_____

_____

_____

_____

_____

_____

DATE: _____

KID: .... AGE: ....

PLACE: ....

WHAT THEY SAID OR DID: ....

....

....

....

....

....

....

DATE: ....

KID: _____ AGE: _____

PLACE: _____

WHAT THEY SAID OR DID: _____

_____

_____

_____

DATE: _____

KID: _____ AGE: _____

PLACE: _____

WHAT THEY SAID OR DID: _____

_____

_____

_____

DATE: _____

KID: AGE:

PLACE:

WHAT THEY SAID OR DID:

DATE:

KID: AGE:

PLACE:

WHAT THEY SAID OR DID:

DATE:

KID: .... AGE: ....

PLACE: ....

WHAT THEY SAID OR DID: ....

....

....

....

....

....

....

....

....

....

....

DATE: ....

KID: AGE:

PLACE:

WHAT THEY SAID OR DID:

DATE:

KID: AGE:

PLACE:

WHAT THEY SAID OR DID:

DATE:

KID: AGE:

PLACE:

WHAT THEY SAID OR DID:

DATE:

KID: .... AGE: ....

PLACE: ....

WHAT THEY SAID OR DID: ....

....

....

....

....

....

....

....

....

....

DATE: ....

KID: AGE:

PLACE:

WHAT THEY SAID OR DID:

DATE:

KID: _____ AGE: _____

PLACE: _____

WHAT THEY SAID OR DID:

_____

_____

_____

_____

_____

_____

_____

_____

_____

_____

DATE: _____

KID: AGE:

PLACE:

WHAT THEY SAID OR DID:

DATE:

KID: AGE:

PLACE:

WHAT THEY SAID OR DID:

KID: AGE:

PLACE:

WHAT THEY SAID OR DID:

KID: _____ AGE: _____

PLACE: _____

WHAT THEY SAID OR DID: _____

_____

_____

_____

DATE: _____

KID: _____ AGE: _____

PLACE: _____

WHAT THEY SAID OR DID: _____

_____

_____

_____

DATE: _____

KID: **AGE:**

PLACE:

WHAT THEY SAID OR DID:

DATE:

KID: .... AGE: ....

PLACE: ....

WHAT THEY SAID OR DID: ....

....

....

....

....

....

....

....

....

....

....

....

DATE: ....

KID: _____ AGE: _____

PLACE: _____

WHAT THEY SAID OR DID:

_____

_____

_____

_____

_____

_____

_____

_____

_____

_____

DATE: _____

KID: AGE:

PLACE:

WHAT THEY SAID OR DID:

DATE: